101 Property Tax Secrets Revealed 2013/14

By

Jennifer Adams

How to beat the taxman and boost your income

Publisher Details

This guide is published by Tax Insider Ltd, 3 Sanderson Close, Warrington WA5 3LN.

'101 Property Tax Secrets Revealed' first published in November 2012, second edition May 2013.

Contents

Contents

Chapter 4.   Income Expenses

Chapter 5.   Capital Allowances

Chapter 10. Minimising Inheritance Tax And The Use Of Trusts

Chapter 11. Minimising Stamp Duty Land Tax

About This Guide

Anyone owning a property will, at some time or other, find themselves subject to tax on that property. If the property is rented out income tax may be payable, on sale possibly capital gains tax and/or stamp duty land tax charged, whilst on death inheritance tax may be levied.

However, there is much that can be done to save or at least reduce the actual amount of tax payable. This guide contains 101 tax savings tips relating specifically to property.

The text follows the lifecycle of the ownership of a property starting with the different ways a property can be owned and financed, and goes on to consider the tax saving possibilities should the property be rented, ending with tax planning ideas on sale or inheritance, including the use of trusts.

It should be noted that the tips in this guide are for illustration purposes only and are intended to demonstrate where tax savings may be made. Any tax savings that are made will be dependent upon the precise circumstances of the situation and the examples are included as a guide only.

It must be stressed that professional advice should always be sought when undertaking any form of tax planning.

Chapter 1.
Business Structure

1.   Sole Investor

A 'sole investor' is an individual who buys properties in his own name. The investor is taxed on any profits made on letting income received and any capital gain made on sale.

Non-tax reasons for buying property as a sole investor:

- You have no partner with whom to share the investment.
- You wish to keep control of your investment, making your own decisions without having to consult another.

Tax reasons for buying property as a sole investor:

- You have no other income, allowing the annual personal allowance to be deducted from any profit made on the letting income in full.
- The share of profit earned on the letting of property owned in joint names is taxed at the respective owner's highest rate of tax. Should one owner be a non- or basic rate taxpayer and the other a higher or additional rate taxpayer then that owner's share of the profit will be taxed at the higher rates.

Sole Investor

Joanne and Robert own a rental property 50:50. Joanne has no other income but Robert is a 45% (additional) rate taxpayer. Net rental profit is £750 per month – £9,000 per tax year.

Joanne: No tax liability as £9,000 x 50% = £4,500 (less than the personal allowance of £9,440).

Robert: Tax liability of £2,025 (£4,500 @ 45%).

If Joanne owned the property in her own name as a sole investor there would be no tax liability on the full profit (£9,000 being less than the personal allowance). This would result in a tax saving of £2,025.

2.   Joint Investors

A joint investment/partnership exists when two or more persons own property that is let out. The individual partners are taxed on their share of the annual profits or gains made – not on their drawings.

Non-tax reasons for buying as joint investors/ partnership:

- You wish to share the investment.
- You wish to share the control and running of the properties.
- On death you wish the property to be transferred automatically to the partner who may not be your next of kin.
- You are not able to fund the investment on your own.

Tax reasons for buying as joint investors/ partnership:

- You are a higher or additional rate taxpayer and your partner(s) is a basic rate or a non-taxpayer(s). Correct tax planning can enable a reduction of the total tax bill.

Joint Investors

Joanne and Robert own a portfolio of rental properties 50:50.

Joanne is a basic rate taxpayer but Robert is a 45% additional rate taxpayer. Total net rental profit is £750 per month i.e. £9,000 per year = £4,500 each.

Joanne: Tax liability of £900 (£4,500 @20%).

Robert: Tax liability of £2,025 (£4,500 @ 45%).

If Robert owned the properties as a sole investor the tax liability would be £4,050; by owning the properties jointly with Joanne there is a tax saving of £1,125.

3.   Limited Liability Partnerships

A Limited Liability Partnership (LLP) is a corporate body with its own legal personality.

It must be registered at Companies House and have a minimum of two 'members'. Each partnership member is taxable on the income they derive from the LLP. A company can be a member of an LLP.

Non-tax reasons for buying property as an LLP:

- It is a legal body separate from its members.
- The members are protected from the acts of other members, not having joint liability as for a general partnership.

Tax reasons for buying property as an LLP:

- Different tax rates between members.

4. Profit Allocation

A property owned jointly or in partnership does not necessarily mean that the rental profit or loss must be allocated in the same proportion as the underlying ownership of the property. The owners can agree a different split as they see fit, the proportion referring to profits and losses only and not to the capital received should the property be sold.

It would be advisable for there to be an agreement quite separate from the property purchase deed that confirms the proportion.

The agreement could accommodate any change in the owners' circumstances on an annual basis (for example) and thus ensure that the personal allowance and different tax rates are used to the best advantage each year.

Profit Allocation

The purchase deed of 54 Dorchester Place shows that the property ownership is split 90:10 between John and his partner, Jane. The net rental profit is £7,200 per year. John is a higher rate taxpayer whilst Jane is a student with no income other than her share of the profit.

John's annual tax bill is £2,592 on his 90% share (£7,200 x 90% @ 40% = £2,592); Jane has no tax to pay on her 10% share (£7,200 x 10% = £720 – less than the personal allowance).

Joint net amount remaining after tax = £7,200 – £2,592 = £4,608.

It would be more beneficial for the 90:10 split to be in Jane's favour as this would mean a tax bill for John of £288 and nil for Jane.

Joint net amount remaining after tax = £7,200 – £288 = £6,912.

There would be a tax saving of £2,304.

5.   Company

There are different types of companies but the one most commonly used for property tax planning is the private company limited by shares. Shareholders are the owners of the company which is administered by directors. Property can be owned by a limited company which has just one shareholder/director.

Non-tax reasons for buying as a company:

- a limited company is a separate legal entity from the shareholders;
- profits and losses belong to the company;
- the company can continue regardless of the death, resignation or bankruptcy of the shareholders or directors;
- the liability of shareholders is limited to the amount unpaid (if any) on the shares held;
- if the company fails, the shareholders are not normally required to make good the deficit (unless personal guarantees have been given);
- suppliers may be more ready to give credit to a company than to a sole trader or partnership;
- a company may find it easier to raise finance.

Tax reason for buying as a company:

The 'small profits rate' for a company is 20% on profits up to £300,000. Although companies do not have a personal allowance, if the net rental profits from a property business are taxed at the higher rates of tax as an individual, it would potentially be more beneficial for the properties to be held inside a company.

6.   Dealer Or Investor?

Difference

Someone buying property to let out on a long-term basis is deemed to be an investor, whereas someone buying property to refurbish then sell, whether resulting in a gain or not, will most likely be deemed to be dealing or trading in properties – the main factor being *intention*.

Capital/investment transaction

Unless losses are incurred on sale it is usually preferable for a transaction to be of a capital/investment nature and for the property to be held personally or via a joint/partnership investment, rather than held within a company. This is because individuals are allowed an annual exempt amount on sale and invariably are charged a lower rate of capital gains tax than the tax rates charged on company profits.

Investment property does not qualify for Business Property Relief when considering inheritance tax.

Property dealing/trading transaction

If the transaction is in a property dealing/trading situation and the property owner is taxed at the higher rates, it may be preferable for the property to be owned instead within a company because the overall tax rates charged through corporate ownership can be lower than the income tax rates.

7.　Record Keeping

UK-resident landlords are generally taxed on rental profits made wherever the properties are situated in the world.

A record of the rental income, expenses incurred and capital items purchased must be kept. Separate sets of records are needed if the properties are let as 'furnished holiday lets' (see Tip 33) because these properties are taxed under different tax rules.

Keep:

- invoices, expense and capital item receipts, rental statements;
- past years' income and expenditure accounts and Tax Returns submitted;
- bank statements;
- details of purchase of property – date of acquisition, purchase price including associated costs; and
- if the property was previously the landlord's main residence, details of periods when the landlord lived in the property and of periods let – to ensure Principal Private Residence and letting relief are correctly claimed on sale.

Record Keeping

Keep records manually, using spreadsheets, or use software packages, for example 'Landlords Property Manager'.

HMRC have an index of the record-keeping requirements for a business at www.hmrc.gov.uk/recordkeeping/index.htm.

A penalty of up to £3,000 can be imposed by HMRC for failure to maintain adequate records for self-assessment purposes.

Chapter 2.
Property Ownership

8.   Ownership

Persons who own property on their own do so in their sole name with sole rights.

Spouses/civil partners can own property in their own names or joint names.

The two legal ways in which property can be held jointly are:

- Joint tenants – each owner has equal rights over the property; when one dies the property is automatically transferred into the other owner's name.
- Tenants in common – the share of each owner is separate, may be unequal and may be disposed of in lifetime or on death as the respective owner wishes.

9. Joint Spouse/Civil Partnership Ownership (1)

By default, rental profit from property jointly owned by spouses/civil partners is taxed 50:50 irrespective of the underlying respective proportion of actual ownership. (This does not apply to property held within a partnership proper.)

However, if it would be more income tax efficient for the split of profit to be different, then the profit may be split according to actual ownership once HMRC has been notified. A couple may also change the underlying ownership to suit but note that such unequal ownership can only be achieved as 'tenants in common'.

Most importantly, a form 17 *'Declaration of beneficial interest in joint property and income'* must be filed with HMRC within 60 days of the date of signature (this restriction is strictly applied).

The declaration will come into effect from the date of signature (i.e. it cannot be back dated) and remains in place until a replacement form is submitted. A replacement form will be required either when the interests in the property or income change, or the owners stop living together as a married couple/civil partners.

Evidence of beneficial interests in the property being unequal must be submitted with the signed form in all cases (e.g. the signing of a declaration of trust or a deed of arrangement).

Joint Spouse/Civil Partnership Ownership (1)

Andrew and Anne are married and jointly own a rented property. Andrew is a 45% additional rate taxpayer and Anne is a 20% basic rate taxpayer. Their accountant has calculated that it would be more beneficial for the profit to be split 80:20 to ensure that the least income tax is paid.

The legal ownership is therefore changed to being held 80:20 as 'tenants in common' and the declaration form 17 signed, but unfortunately was not submitted within the 60-day time limit.

The income tax split therefore remains at 50:50 but legally the underlying ownership has changed to 80:20. The 50:50 tax split will remain until a fresh Form 17 is submitted.

10. Joint Spouse/Civil Partnership Ownership (2)

If one spouse/civil partner owns rented properties solely in their own name but is a higher or additional rate taxpayer and the other spouse/civil partner is not, it would be beneficial for at least some of the rental profit to be taxed on the spouse/civil partner.

To alter the income tax percentage charged, ownership of part of the property must be transferred into the other spouse/civil partner's name.

Should the owning spouse/civil partner not wish to transfer any material percentage ownership but still wishes to reduce their tax bill, a nominal amount of, say, 1% could be transferred.

In this instance the HMRC form 17 *'Declaration of beneficial interest in joint property and income'* must **not** be signed because not signing will ensure that the underlying property ownership is (say) 99:1 but the income split is 50:50.

Joint Spouse Ownership (2)

Andrew and Anne are married. Andrew owns a property yielding £8,000 annually. Andrew is a 45% additional rate taxpayer and Anne a non-taxpayer.

Andrew transfers 1% of the property ownership to Anne, retaining 99%. Each will be taxed on 50% of the income. As Anne is a non-taxpayer this will produce a tax saving of £1,800.

11. Joint Non-Spouse/Civil Partnership Ownership

If a property is owned jointly by two persons who are not married or in a civil partnership, the rental profit is **not** automatically split 50:50.

Rather, the income split is in whatever proportion they agree between themselves.

The HMRC form 17 *'Declaration of beneficial interest in joint property and income'* is **not** relevant in this instance but a written agreement would be helpful.

12.   Agreements On Transfer

The transfer of a share in a property business is confirmed by the signing of a written agreement.

To enable a transfer to take place the property needs to be held by the partners as 'tenants in common', thus ensuring that each partner's share can be disposed of to whomever and in whatever proportion each wishes. The income split will be a separate matter being in whatever proportions the partners agree between themselves.

Agreements on Transfer

Jack and Jill are married and jointly own a BTL property, with no mortgage. They wish to gift 1% of the property to each of their two *adult* children (new share of property being 49:49:1:1), the rental income and expenses to be shared 50:50 between the adult children only. What are the practicalities?

If the property is held as 'tenants in common' Jack and Jill can each transfer 1%; one percent to one child and one percent to the other. Two written agreements will be needed, one to confirm each transfer. The amendment to the net profit allocation should also be confirmed.

There will be no stamp duty land tax on the transfer as each transfer is a gift with no consideration. There will possibly be no CGT due either as although the gifts will be deemed to have taken place at market value, with such a small percentage of ownership being transferred, the value may well be less than the annual exempt amounts.

Chapter 3.
Finance And Investment

13.   Allowable Interest

Any business owner taking out a mortgage in order to finance capital to invest in a business is allowed to deduct the interest paid from income received.

The renting out of property is deemed to be a 'business' in the taxman's eyes for income tax purposes; the 'capital' investment being the property itself, therefore mortgage interest is deductible from rental income.

Should an owner of a property business not use all of the available mortgage capital, the interest remains fully allowable (assuming that what is used, is used only for business purposes) because the original reason for the mortgage remains, namely to invest capital in the business in order to finance the purchase of property.

14.   Equity Release

Interest paid on a mortgage taken out to release capital in a rented property can still be deducted from the rental profit received from that property should the capital raised then be used to purchase another property or even to reduce the capital outstanding on the main residence. The actual reason for the mortgage is not important.

The key criterion is that the total amount of capital released must not exceed the market value of the property when originally brought into the letting business. If the property had originally been bought for letting then this amount would be the purchase price; otherwise use the market value at the date of transfer.

Equity Release

Anne wishes to raise £150,000 via a mortgage on two BTL properties that were purchased with cash some years ago. The purchase price of the properties was £125,000 and they were let out immediately on acquisition. The mortgage monies will be used as capital to purchase a holiday cottage for personal use.

The maximum amount of interest allowable will be the proportion relating to the amount paid for the properties originally, i.e. £125,000.

There is no need to include the cottage in the portfolio for tax relief to be allowed; it can be kept for private use but interest on £25,000 will be disallowed.

15.   Portfolio Mortgages

Tax relief is allowed on interest paid on mortgages/loans taken out to finance the purchase of assets held within a business. Landlords who own two or more properties are deemed to own a 'portfolio' of business assets.

Lenders have designed products that treat the 'portfolio' as one single business account regardless of the number of properties purchased or whether the full amount of capital has been utilised. The individual properties may have separate mortgages each with different interest rates charged but the 'portfolio' is treated as one single business account.

One portfolio means one agreement, one monthly payment and one mortgage statement.

Should not all of the capital be used, tax relief on interest payments made remains fully allowable because the original reason for the mortgage/loan remains – namely to finance the use of capital by a property business.

Portfolio Mortgages

Avril owns six properties with a total value of £2m. With a portfolio mortgage outstanding of £1.7m there is a 'shortfall' of £300,000. This amount is not the equity found in any one property but in the portfolio spread over the six properties. This allows £300,000 for further investment; the interest will be fully tax deductible.

16.   Personal Loans

Interest on personal loans taken out for business purposes is deductible from rental income received.

Examples:

- Mortgage providers currently require a deposit of at least 20% of a property's value before lending the remaining 80%. If the 20% is not available, the owner can finance via a personal loan and the interest paid will be fully allowable.
- Should refurbishment or other building work be required, interest paid on a personal loan to finance the work will be fully allowable.
- If the property is to be rented fully furnished or as a Furnished Holiday Let, items such as a cooker and a fridge will be required. These items can be purchased on loans repayable over a period (usually 6 or 12 months) and the interest paid on these loans is also fully allowable.

Personal Loans

Bill is refurbishing a number of properties in his portfolio but has a cash-flow problem. He will be unable to pay his builders at the end of the week. He knows that the shortfall will be temporary and therefore applies for a short-term loan from the bank.

The interest charged is 12% but the interest paid will be allowable in full against the rental income as the loan has been incurred for the purpose of running his business.

17.   Cash Then Mortgage

Interest rates on mortgages are at an all-time low but there are reasons why using available cash to purchase a property rather than taking out a mortgage may be necessary or beneficial.

Use Cash

- When you can secure a discount on purchase by doing so.
- If by not paying cash the sale will fall through – mortgages can take weeks to materialise.
- When the rental profit exceeds interest payments with sufficient remaining to prove that the return on the cash invested is greater than if the money had remained in a savings account.

Then Mortgage, If Necessary

If cash is used to finance the purchase initially and then the property is mortgaged to replace the cash, the interest paid on the mortgage will be allowable in full against the rental income when received. The reason for the interest payments being allowed is 'intention' – the intention all along was to purchase the property via a mortgage; the cash is being used merely in place of a bridging loan.

Chapter 4.
Income Expenses

18. Revenue v Capital Expenditure

In calculating the profit or loss of a rental business the on-going costs of renting a property (agents' fees, repairs, insurance, etc.) being 'revenue costs' are allowable immediately as a deduction against rental income received.

No deductions are allowed for capital expenditure but capital allowances may be claimed to take into account the depreciation of some capital assets used.

Ascertaining whether a cost is a revenue or capital expense can be difficult but HMRC have published a Toolkit which is in the format of questions to help in deciding under which heading the expenditure is to be allowed.

Revenue v Capital Expenditure

HMRC Toolkit weblink:
www.hmrc.gov.uk/agents/toolkits/capital-v-revenue.pdf

19. 'Duality Of Purpose'

Expenses incurred in the running of a property business are deductible from rental income received in calculating the taxable profit. However, just because a payment has been made does not necessarily mean that it will be allowable.

Strictly, for an expense to be allowed the business purpose must be the sole purpose; there must be no dual reason for the expense. Where it is difficult to split the business element from any private element then the whole expense amount is usually disallowed.

In practice, however, some 'dual purpose'-type expenses may be allowed. The expense most usually quoted is where a car is used partly for business and partly for private purposes during the year, the business part obviously being allowed.

Duality of Purpose

James rents out his former main residence in Manchester whilst he is working away from home in Brighton. Every month he travels by car to Manchester to view the property.

There is a 'duality of purpose' in the motoring expenses such that a proportion of the petrol, oil, etc. would be disallowed as being incurred for personal use.

20. Foreign Travel Expenses

The cost of business-related travel in attending to rental properties is allowable as an expense for tax purposes; any travel costs incurred for personal reasons are not.

Travel costs in attending foreign let property can also be claimed providing that there is no 'duality of purpose' (i.e. that you visited the property whilst also on holiday).

Foreign Travel Expenses

John owns a portfolio of properties in the UK and Spain. He is interested in expanding his portfolio into Portugal.

Whilst on holiday in Spain he visits the Spanish property for its annual visit and also flies to Portugal to view the potential property before flying back to Spain to finish his holiday. He then returns to the UK from Spain.

The travel costs of car parking, petrol, flight to Spain and then back to the UK will not be allowed as there is a 'duality of purpose' of the holiday.

The similar costs of the flight, etc. from Spain to Portugal will be allowed in full as being incurred solely in relation to the rental business.

21.   Car Expenses

The cost of running a vehicle used in a letting business can be claimed against rental income in full. Unless the vehicle is used solely for business purposes the costs must be apportioned between private and business use.

There are two methods of calculation:

1.   Note the recorded mileage on 6 April each year giving the total mileage over the full tax year. Record the mileage of every business-related trip made in the tax year, which will give the proportion of running costs to claim.
2.   A business with annual turnover of less than the VAT registration limit (currently £79,000) can claim 45p for the first 10,000 business miles incurred and 25p for any additional miles.

Whichever method is used, once used, it cannot be changed until the vehicle itself is changed.

Car Expenses

Susan travels 12,000 miles on business attending to her portfolio of properties. The recorded mileage for the year is 15,000. Total cost of running the car is £3,750 per year.

Method 1 : £3,750 x 12,000/15,000 = £3,000

Method 2: (10,000 x 45p) + (2,000 x 25p) = £5,000

Method 2 will produce the most tax-efficient amount to claim.

22. Legal Fees

Expenditure on professional fees is deductible from the rental income of a property as revenue expenditure if incurred for the purposes of the rental business. Expenses incurred in relation to the purchase and sale of a property are deductible as capital expenditure on disposal of the property in the capital gains tax calculation.

Specific legal costs allowed as revenue expenditure:

- Fees incurred on the renewal of a lease if the lease is for less than 50 years (except for any proportion that relates to the payment of a premium on the renewal of a lease).
- Expenses incurred in connection with the first letting if it is for a tenure of **less** than a year (includes the cost of drawing up the lease, agents' and surveyors' fees and commission).
- Expenses incurred on preparing a replacement short lease where it closely follows a previous agreement.
- Costs in relation to rent arbitration and evicting an unsatisfactory tenant so as to re-let.

Specific legal costs allowed as capital expenditure:

- Generally, costs are deemed to be a capital expense if they relate to a capital item, such as the actual purchase or sale of the property.

23.   'Wear And Tear' Allowance

The 'wear and tear' allowance can only be claimed on rental property let furnished when it includes such items as a cooker, fridge, sofa, etc.

The allowance cannot be claimed on unfurnished or partly furnished properties.

The claim is an annual allowance calculated as 10% of the net rental received after deducting any costs paid for by the landlord which are normally the tenant's burden – such as council tax.

'Wear and Tear' Allowance

John lets out a fully furnished property at a rent of £600 per month. Out of this £600 he pays £100, being the cost of the utility bills and the gardener each month.

John is allowed to claim 'wear and tear' allowance as follows:

Annual income = (£600 – £100 per month) x 12 months = £6,000.

'Wear and tear' allowance claim: £6,000 x 10% = £600.

24.   Tenant Repairing

If a business rents a commercial property and under the terms of the lease is required to incur the cost of repairing part of the property, the expense is allowed against the profits of the tenant's business in full as the cost is required to enable the business to continue.

'Repair' in this context means 'restoration' of an asset by replacing subsidiary parts of the whole property.

If there is a significant improvement of the asset beyond its original condition then that is deemed capital expenditure and depending upon the type of improvement may fall within the capital allowances rules (see Tip 5).

Tenant Repairing

Cerne Books Ltd rents a commercial property and under the terms of the lease is required to undergo specific repairs. Following a storm some tiles came off the roof – the cost of replacing these tiles is deemed a 'repair' and can be deducted from the company's profits as an allowable expense.

25. Pre-Letting Expenses

Expenses may be incurred in the setting up of a letting business (for example, travel, phone, advertising, etc.) before the first rental receipt is received; if so, deduction may be possible once the letting starts.

Relief is only possible under these special rules where the expenditure:

- is incurred within a period of seven years before the date the rental business actually starts; and
- is not otherwise allowable as a deduction for tax purposes (i.e. against any other income or capital); and
- would have been allowed as a deduction if it had been incurred after the rental business started.

Letting expenditure incurred pre-commencement is treated as having been incurred on the day on which the rental business starts and then added to other allowable letting expenses incurred during the tax year. This total amount is then deducted from the total letting receipts for that year.

The expenses must not be for the purchase of capital items. Capital expenditure is potentially deductible but there are separate rules of calculation.

Costs incurred in relation to the actual purchase of the property, including legal fees, are a capital cost allowed against the proceeds of the eventual disposal of property under the capital gains tax rules.

26. Pre-Letting Repairs

Expenses for repair and maintenance incurred prior to the first letting income received may be allowable provided certain conditions are met; namely that:

- the cost is for the replacement of worn or dilapidated items;
- the property was in a fit state of repair for use in the letting business prior to its actually being let;
- the price paid for the property was not substantially reduced to take into account its dilapidated state of repair;
- the purchase price, if reduced, was reduced only to take into account 'normal wear and tear'.

Pre-letting Repairs

The surveyor's report undertaken on the purchase of a property will often include an estimate of the rental income that could be derived from a property; this can be useful evidence that the property was in a 'fit state of repair' before money is spent on repairs.

Alternatively the taking of photographs before repairs are undertaken could be admitted as proof.

27. Post-Letting Expenses

Expenses incurred in the running of a property business will have been spent in order to generate income and as such can be deducted from income received during the year.

When the letting ceases there will be no income against which relief can be claimed. However, by ensuring that any expense is accrued (allowed) for, tax relief is available – the crucial factor is not when the expense is paid or the date on the invoice but when the need for the expense arose.

Post-Letting Expenses

Last year Tony rented a property to a couple who left suddenly without giving notice. When Tony entered the property he found it in need of substantial redecoration and repair. A couple of weeks later a reminder for an unpaid electricity bill arrived. What expenses can be claimed?

Damage to property – as the property had been damaged during a letting period the expense of repair can be claimed.

Electricity bill – the bill is not Tony's legal responsibility but if he is unable to find the whereabouts of the previous tenants he will have to pay in order for the electricity supply not to be cut off. The expense is a cost of the letting and is therefore allowable.

28.   Pre-Sale Expenses

After the decision has been made to sell a rental property, expenses incurred **cannot** be deducted from the rental income that has been received. Although there is no specific legal requirement for written confirmation of the date of the decision, it would be advisable to make a note.

If you have a portfolio of properties, expenses such as stationery, petrol, phone bill, etc. are allowable because, even after a particular property has been sold, you will still be running a business receiving income against which such costs may be deducted.

Repair costs incurred on a property that is in the process of being sold are not generally deductible against the property business letting income. They also cannot be utilised as capital expenditure against the sale proceeds as the cost of *maintaining* a capital asset is not deductible for CGT purposes.

Most importantly, mortgage interest accruing after the last tenant has left and the decision has been made to sell is not tax deductible as the property no longer forms part of the letting business.

29. Property Let 'Rent Free'

Properties let 'rent free' are regarded by HMRC as being tax neutral and outside the scope of the property income tax regime. However, no source of income means no associated deduction for expenses, therefore any expenses that are incurred are lost and cannot be relieved.

Property Let 'Rent Free'

To ensure that the property does not lose its 'business' status it needs to remain available for commercial letting even if the property is being used 'rent free' for a time.

For example, a property will be able to retain its commercial status if an owner can prove that he is actively looking for tenants but has allowed the present tenants to reside 'rent free' whilst looking for replacement paying tenants.

30.   'Rent-A-Room' Relief (1) – Calculation

The 'Rent-A-Room' relief scheme is an optional tax exemption scheme that allows people to receive up to £4,250 per annum gross and not be subject to tax by renting out spare furnished rooms in their only or main home.

The rent can include the provision of meals but HMRC may consider that this amounts to a trade, in which case the usual income and expenditure rules apply to be taxed accordingly.

If the rent received exceeds £4,250, the first £4,250 can be tax free, income tax being paid on the balance.

Rent-a-Room Relief

Julie is a basic rate taxpayer receiving gross income of £5,000 from letting out her spare room to include the provision of breakfast.

She will be taxed as follows:

Gross income	£5,000
Relief	(£4,250)
Balance to be taxed	£750

Tax due at the 20% basic rate is £150 per annum.

31. 'Rent-A-Room' Relief (2) – Choice Of Method Of Calculation

The rules of the 'Rent-A-Room' relief scheme enable the landlord to prepare the usual income and expenditure accounts and then compare the actual expenses incurred with the Rent-A-Room relief. He can then claim whichever is more beneficial.

The comparison can be made year on year and changed to cater for whichever gives the better result.

A landlord has up to one year after 31 January following the end of the tax year to decide which option to use.

Rent-a-Room Relief – (Continued from Tip 30)

In the second year of renting Julie received the same gross amount of £5,000 but incurred costs of £6,000, producing a loss of £(1,000).

Clearly for this year it would be more beneficial to prepare normal property income and expense accounts claiming the loss.

The loss can generally be claimed against other property income – or carried forward and offset against future net profits.

32.   'Rent-a-Room' Relief (3) – Rules

There are set rules for use of the 'Rent-A-Room' relief scheme:

- It applies if the taxpayer also rents out unfurnished rooms in the same property (e.g. a furnished room is let to a lodger but there is also an unfurnished annex let out separately).
- The taxpayer and lodger must occupy the property for at least part of the letting period in each tax year of claim.
- Where the owner moves into a new property leaving the lodger in occupation, the relief will be available only until the end of the letting period in that tax year.
- The £4,250 limit is not reduced if the room is let for less than 12 months. The same amount applies, therefore, even if the room is rented for only one month or just in term time.

33. Furnished Holiday Lettings

For income tax and capital gains tax purposes only the operation of a furnished holiday let (FHL) is deemed to be a business and not a property income investment.

Specific points:

- Accommodation must be available for short-term letting for 210 days in any one tax year and actually be let for 105 days of the year.
- Accommodation should not normally be in the same occupation for a continuous period of 31 days in a period of 155 days in any one tax year. Long-term letting should not exceed 155 days.
- The 'occupation' test can be met by making an election to average periods of occupation of any or all of the FHLs owned.
- Rent must be charged at a market rate.
- The rental profit or losses are kept separate from other non-FHL property, such that losses can only be offset against income of the same FHL business.
- CGT business asset 'roll-over' relief and 'entrepreneurs' relief' are potentially available.
- If the property qualified as a FHL last year but failed to do so this year because the actual occupation days were too low, an election can be made to continue to treat as a FHL this year and potentially next year.

Chapter 5.
Capital Allowances

34. Annual Investment Allowance

In calculating the profit or loss of a rental business no deductions are allowed for capital expenditure but capital allowances may be claimed to take account of the depreciation of some capital assets used.

The Annual Investment Allowance (AIA) is a 100% allowance up to £25,000 of investment in standard plant and machinery. This limit has temporarily increased to **£250,000** for expenditure by reference to the period 1 January 2013 through to 31 December 2014.

Expenditure in excess of the limit is dealt with under the standard 'writing down allowance' rules; any unused AIA is lost. Thus, any expenditure in excess of the AIA amount should be delayed until the next tax year.

Annual Investment Allowance

In May 2013 a company invests £350,000 in refurbishing a substantial apartment block – replacing kitchens, bathrooms and security systems. £250,000 of this amount will be eligible for AIA, the remaining £100,000 receiving tax relief (usually at 18% a year on a decreasing balance basis – see Tip 36) under the writing down allowance rules.

35. Landlord's Energy Savings Allowance

Private residential landlords can claim an immediate 100% allowance of up to £1,500 per dwelling per tax year, when improvements to the energy efficiency of the property are made.

The claim is for:

- loft insulation;
- cavity and solid wall insulation;
- draught proofing;
- hot water supply insulation;
- floor insulation.

Conditions:

- The allowance cannot be claimed if 'rent-a-room' relief is claimed on that particular property.
- Not possible to claim on commercial or furnished holiday let accommodation.
- The allowance is applied per dwelling rather than per building so for a house converted into three flats the maximum allowance is £4,500.
- The claim is for expenditure incurred before 1 April 2015 for corporate landlords and 6 April 2015 for individual landlords.
- The allowance is separate from the annual investment allowance.
- The allowance is available on an existing dwelling only.

36. Writing Down Allowance (1) – Sale Of 'Pool' Assets

Capital allowances are available on the purchase of certain fixed asset items used in a letting business.

Expenditure in excess of the Annual Investment Allowance limit is transferred into a 'pool' and claimed ('written down') over a period of several years (generally at 18% per annum).

If any assets in the pool are subsequently sold, the proceeds are deducted from the pool amount brought forward before reducing the value against which further writing down allowances can be claimed.

Writing Down Allowance – Sale of 'Pool' Assets

The brought forward balance on the capital allowances pool claim in Jane's property portfolio as at 31 March 2013 was £85,000.

Assets comprising the main pool were sold for £20,000 during the year 2013/2014. The calculation claim is:

Pool balance brought forward	£85,000
Sale of assets	£(20,000)
Balance	£65,000
Writing down allowance (18%)	£(11,700)
Balance of allowances carried forward	£53,300
Total allowances claimed	£11,700

37. Writing Down Allowance (2) – Excess Expenditure

Where the Annual Investment Allowance (AIA) is not claimed or not available because the limit has already been reached, tax relief is given on the purchase of capital items on a reducing balance termed the 'writing down allowance'.

Expenditure in excess of the AIA limit enters either the main pool (or a 'special rate' pool for the purchase of integrated features) and is eligible for the writing down allowance at 18% per annum (main pool) or 8% ('special rate' pool) in the accounting period.

Writing Down Allowance – Excess Expenditure

In 2013 Jane is granted planning permission to refurbish a block of flats in her portfolio of properties. At the end of the previous accounting period (5 April 2013) there was a main pool balance carried forward of £100,000. The cost of the items totalled £330,000 – all of which is expenditure eligible for the main pool rate of 18%.

Pool balance brought forward	£100,000
Additions qualifying for AIA	£330,000
AIA claim maximum	(£250,000)
Balance allocated to main pool	£80,000
Total eligible for writing down allowance	£180,000
Writing down allowance (18%)	£(32,400)
Balance of allowances carried forward	£147,600

Total allowances claimed: £250,000 + £32,400 = £282,400

38.   Restricted Claim

Capital allowances available on assets purchased for use in a property business need not be claimed in full; the amount can be restricted by choice, if appropriate.

This will be relevant if, for example, the owner's total income for the year is less than the personal allowance.

The amount of allowances claimed in any one year can be restricted to bring the profit to the level of the personal allowance, thereby preserving the balance of allowances to be carried forward for future years.

Restricted Claim

Jane's property business has a main pool written down value brought forward of £80,000. Profit for the year to 31 March 2014 is £18,000; she has no other income.

The tax calculation is:

Pool balance brought forward	£80,000
Writing down allowance possible at 18%	£14,400
Amount of claim (restricted)	£(8,560)
Balance of allowances carried forward	£71,440

Tax liability calculation:

Profit	£18,000
Less writing down allowance claim	£(8,560)
Net profit	£9,440
Personal Allowance 2013/2014	£(9,440)
Tax liability	NIL

39. 'Special Rate' Allowance

Special rules apply for the claiming of capital allowances on the purchase of 'integral features' which comprise the following relevant to property lettings:

- electrical system, including a lighting system;
- cold water system;
- heating system, a powered system of ventilation, air cooling or air purification, and any floor or ceiling in such a system;
- lift or escalator; or
- external solar heating.

Any item not on the list, even if it forms part of the building, is outside the scope of the integral features rules. Expenditure on such assets in excess of any claim under the Annual Investment Allowance (AIA) is allocated to a 'special rate' pool of 8% on a written down balance.

'Special Rate' Allowance

Diana spends a total of £14,000 on 'integral features' for her properties. The AIA limit has already been exceeded for the period and writing down allowances (WDA) need to be claimed. The expenditure is allocated to the 'special rate' pool.

Additions:	
Electrical lighting system	£10,000
Air conditioning	£4,000
	£14,000
WDA at 8%	£(1,120)
Balance of allowances carried forward	£12,880
Total allowances claim	£1,120

40.   Vehicles

If a van is used in the letting business to travel between properties or from office to property, the purchase cost of the van is allowed in full under the Annual Investment Allowance (AIA).

AIA is not available for a claim on cars; cars attract a writing down allowance (WDA) of 18% per annum, or 8% if the vehicle's CO_2 emissions exceed 160g/km.

For capital allowances claims, the claim can only represent a proportion of business use of the asset – private use being disallowed.

However, if a car owned by a company is required to be garaged on company premises overnight with private use essentially being forbidden, then the whole WDA is allowed against the company's profits.

It is difficult to claim the full WDA successfully on a car owned by an individual because HMRC will normally argue that the car must be used privately to some extent.

Vehicles

David purchased a car a couple of years ago and in April 2013 started to use it in his business – the car's value is £5,000 with CO_2 emissions of 165g/km. He calculates that the car is used 75% of the time on business.

The WDA claim for 2013/2014 is calculated as £5,000 x 8% x 75% = £300. The amount carried forward to 2013/2014 = £4,600 (i.e. £5,000 – £400, being the total WDA before restricting for private use).

41. Business Premises Renovation Allowance

The Business Premises Renovation Allowance (BPRA) allows 100% capital allowances to be claimed on the cost of conversion of derelict or unused business premises – dependent upon specific conditions being met. One condition is that relief is only available for renovating or converting disused business premises in what is designated a 'disadvantaged area' (as specified in the Assisted Areas Order 2007).

If the conditions are not met or the full allowance not claimed then a writing down allowance is available at 25% annually (25% of the initial qualifying expenditure) on a straight-line basis.

There is a 'balancing charge' adjustment if a specific 'balancing event' occurs within seven years, e.g. sale of property. The balancing charge will arise if proceeds received exceed the amount of allowance claimed.

Business Premises Renovation Allowance

Emily buys a derelict shop and renovates it, converting it into a cafe. The renovation costs £150,000 for which she makes a claim for 100% relief. After four years she sells the cafe for £200,000 – the sale is deemed a 'balancing event' as it occurs within seven years.

A 'balancing charge' arises – the residue on sale is nil as all of the allowance has been claimed. The proceeds of sale exceed the initial claim so the charge is capped at £150,000.

NOTE: The 'take up' for this scheme has been so good that HMRC has extended the scheme to April 2017.

42. Ancillary Expenses

When a property business undertakes expenditure that is capital in nature such that a capital allowance is claimed, that cost can be augmented by 'ancillary' expenses.

Such ancillary expenses include labour and material expenses paid to install an item of plant or equipment plus costs of structural alterations to a building to accommodate the new plant.

Professional fees paid to architects or structural engineers can also be claimed provided it can be proved that the costs relate directly to the installation of the plant and machinery.

Ancillary Expenses

The availability of tax relief on ancillary expenses produces a tax planning possibility.

Tony bought a commercial building but after an inspection was advised to install a lift. A lift is eligible for capital allowances but the actual lift shaft is considered to be part of the building. If the lift had been installed at the time of building, the cost of the lift shaft would be ineligible for capital allowances and as such is not relievable until the sale of the building as a CGT cost.

However, as Tony has decided to install the lift *after* the building has been built the lift shaft becomes ancillary to the installation of qualifying machinery, is an ancillary cost and as such is allowable for capital allowances.

43. Sale Of Commercial Property – s198 Claim (1)

When a commercial property is sold, part of the selling price will include the value of fixtures which have qualified for capital allowances in the seller's business. If the proceeds of sale on those assets exceed the written down value of the 'pool' there will be a 'balancing charge' which is treated as a negative allowance and capital allowances previously claimed will be clawed back.

A 's198 claim' can be made between the two parties that enables them to agree a value for capital allowances purposes only, not exceeding the original purchase price of the assets. Post April 2012 a s198 claim to submit to HMRC will effectively be mandatory in most cases (see Tip 44).

The seller will want to set a value as low as possible to maximise allowances but the purchaser will want to agree a value that enables him to make some amount of claim carrying forward.

Sale of Commercial Property – s198 Claim (1)

Steve sells an industrial unit to Fred. He originally purchased it in 2007 for £250,000 and the agreed price is £300,000. Steve has claimed capital allowances on air conditioning and security systems costing £50,000. If the written down value of the assets was £20,000 and the proceeds value restricted to £50,000, £30,000 allowances that Steve has previously claimed will be 'clawed' back.

If the value agreed under the election is £100, Steve will be able to claim a balancing allowance on sale of £19,900 but Fred will only be able to claim £100 going forward.

44. Sale Of Commercial Property – s198 Claim (2)

The tax rules state that the purchaser's entitlement to capital allowances in relation to a commercial property purchase is restricted to the disposal value that the past owner of the property brought into account, even if this was not the immediate past owner. Furthermore, it is the purchaser's responsibility to obtain and provide details of prior claims and disposal values, which might prove difficult if the original owner has ceased trading or if records are no longer available.

Post April 2012, should a s198 election agreement not be entered into (or a decision not sought from the Tribunal), any future rights of claim to these capital allowances will be lost not only to the immediate purchaser but also to any future owner of the property.

Sale of Commercial Property - 's198 Claim' (2)

In the tax case of **Mr and Mrs Tapsell and Mr Lester as partnership The Granleys**, the partners purchased a care home as a going concern of which £40,000 was allocated to 'fixtures and fittings'; they made a claim for capital allowances thereon of £146,014. This figure was based on an apportionment of £106,014 relating to the purchase of the plant and machinery fixtures in the property plus £40,000 as shown in the contract.

Shortly afterwards, the sellers submitted a capital allowances claim for £68,811 for the same tax year. They provided no supporting details to HMRC; they then emigrated and could not be traced by either the purchasers or HMRC.

HMRC disallowed the purchasers' capital allowances claim on the grounds that they failed to show that the same expenditure on plant and machinery had not been claimed by the sellers.

Chapter 6.
Using Losses

45. Losses

Losses from a property business are calculated in the same way as losses from a trade.

The loss on one property in a portfolio is automatically offset against profits made on any other properties in the same portfolio for the same period.

Therefore profits and losses of all UK properties are 'pooled' together. As profits and losses of any overseas properties are kept separate, two distinct and separate 'pools' are created should there be both UK and foreign properties in a portfolio.

Losses on furnished holiday lettings (FHLs) are also kept separate and cannot be offset against either other UK rental profits or profits made on foreign properties. They too are 'pooled': a UK FHL property 'pool' and a separate overseas FHL 'pool'.

Losses

Joan owns two properties – one in France and one in London.

She lets out both properties in 2013/14 – the London one for the full year but the one in France for only two months over the summer. She makes a net profit on the property in London but a net loss on the one in France. Neither constitutes a FHL.

The loss on the French property cannot be offset against the profits made on the London property and must be kept separate; however, the loss can be carried forward and deducted against any profit made in future lettings of the French property – or indeed any other overseas non-FHL properties she might subsequently acquire.

46. Losses Carried Forward

If there is an overall income tax loss made for a tax year, that loss is generally relieved as follows:

- Carried forward and set against profits made in future years on properties in the same UK property business (or if overseas property, against the same overseas property business).
- Losses from UK furnished holiday lettings (FHLs) can only be carried forward and set against profits made on other UK FHL properties. The losses cannot be deducted from profits made on other lettings (including profits made on an overseas FHL business).
- If the loss arises on cessation, relief may be possible as being set against the owners' general income, or against capital gains made in certain circumstances.
- The above rules apply for income tax purposes. For companies, property losses may normally be set against total profits of that or following accounting periods, or 'group relieved'.

Losses Carried Forward

Ben owns a portfolio of four properties (none of which is a FHL). Together a loss was incurred for the year 2012/13 but a profit for the year 2013/2014. His other income makes him a basic rate taxpayer.

Calculation:

2012/13	Loss carried forward	£(20,000)
2013/14	Profit	£10,000
Loss carried forward to 2014/15		£(10,000)

Nil tax due on lettings for either year 2012/13 or 2013/14.

47.   Offsetting Losses

If there is an overall income tax loss on an individual's (not a company's) continuing property portfolio over a tax year and that loss has been created by excess capital allowances claimed, then that loss can be relieved by being offset against the owner's other ('general') income for the same and/or next tax year. Otherwise the loss is automatically carried forward and set against future profits of the same UK property business.

You would offset the loss against other income for the same and/or next tax year if you have taxable income in excess of the personal allowance. Otherwise better tax planning would be to carry forward the loss, such as not to waste the loss against income already covered by the personal allowance – remember also that capital allowances can be disclaimed (restricted) to suit. The loss can be set against the current year, or the next year, or both if large enough. Any unutilised loss is carried forward for offset against future rental profits.

Offsetting Losses

Ben owns a portfolio of four properties. He purchased capital assets and claimed Annual Investment Allowance thereon producing an overall loss of £10,000. If he is a taxpayer with income in excess of the personal allowance he can claim for the loss to be offset, thereby reducing his taxable income resulting in a possible tax refund.

If he has no other income the loss should be carried forward and offset against profits of the future period, if any.

48. Dormant Periods

Losses from a rental business can only be set against future profits if the business is a continuing business.

In some instances it will not be clear as to whether a property business has ceased as the rental activities may stop and then restart. HMRC apply a general ruling by which they regard the 'old' business as ceasing if there is a gap of at least **three years** between lets and different properties are let in the taxpayer's old and new letting activities.

Thus, a business is not normally treated as having ceased simply because the property is not let for a period to allow for repairs or renovations.

However, the property business may be treated as having ceased and then recommencing should the property be used as the taxpayer's main residence between lets.

The losses of a ceased property business cannot be set against the profits of a 'new' property business.

49.   Cessation Of Business

Where the property business of a sole trader or partnership has ceased, a post-cessation relief allowing offset against current income may be available where, within seven years of the business ceasing, the taxpayer is required to make a '**qualifying**' **payment** or an '**event**' has occurred in connection with the ceased business.

- 'Qualifying' payment is for the remedying of defective work and legal expenses in connection with such defects.

- 'Qualifying' event is the confirmation of unpaid debts taken into account in calculating the profits or losses of the business.

The maximum must be offset against income first and then the balance may be relieved against any capital gains accruing in the same year.

Cessation of Business

Dawn sold the last property in her portfolio on 25 July 2007. In January 2014 she loses a court case for defective services and is obliged to make a compensation payment of £10,000. Her P60 for 2013/2014 shows taxable income of £30,000.

If she makes a claim by 31 January 2016 she can offset the £10,000 against her 2013/2014 income and obtain a tax refund.

50. Capital Losses – Negligible Value

Tax relief is available when an asset is lost, destroyed or becomes of negligible value – this is possible, for example, when a BTL property is purchased 'off plan', the builder goes into liquidation, money is lost and the property never built.

To claim the relief:

- The investor must still own the property when it becomes of negligible value.
- The amount of relief is calculated as if the property had been sold and immediately reacquired.
- The claim can be made for an earlier time in the previous two tax years in which the deemed disposal occurred (see example) or for companies, any accounting period ending not more than two years before the date of the claim.
- The claim is not automatic and needs to be claimed on the Tax Return.

Capital Losses – Negligible Value

In November 2010 Fred entered into an agreement with a developer to buy two flats 'off plan' for £200,000 per flat. A deposit of 10% per flat was paid plus legal fees of £3,500. Fred received a letter in January 2013 stating that the developer had gone into liquidation. In January 2014 it is confirmed that the development will not be going ahead and that Fred will not be receiving repayment of the deposit.

The loss of £(43,500) ((£200,000 x 2 x 10%) + £3,500) is treated as a normal capital loss for either offset against other gains made during the same year of claim or carried forward against future gains.

The offset could apply for the tax year as early as 2012/2013 on the basis that that was the year in which the money was 'lost'.

51. Capital Losses – Negligible Value – Spouse/Civil Partners

Tax planning possibility:

- Disposals between spouses/civil partners are deemed to occur on a 'no gain/no loss' basis.
- If one spouse/civil partner owns an asset which on sale has produced a capital gain in excess of the annual exempt amount and the other spouse/civil partner has an asset standing at a potential negligible-value loss, the negligible value asset can be transferred to the spouse/civil partner, the loss offset and capital gain reduced.

Capital Losses – Negligible Value – Spouses

Fred has a negligible-value asset standing at loss of £43,500 but his wife has sold property owned in her own name producing capital gains totalling £60,000.

If Fred was to transfer the loss-making asset to his wife, she could offset the loss against the gains made and receive a reduced CGT bill.

Chapter 7.
Foreign Matters

52. Non-Resident Landlord Scheme – Tax Planning

The 'Non-Resident Landlord Scheme' (NRLS) is a scheme for taxing the UK rental income of non-resident landlords. Usually basic rate tax is deducted from the net rent collected by an agent (less expenses paid) or paid by a tenant unless the agent/tenant has authority from HMRC under the NRLS to pay the landlord gross.

'Non-resident landlords' under this scheme are persons (individuals, companies, trustees) who are in receipt of UK rental income, and whose **'usual place of abode'** is outside of the UK.

Although the scheme refers to 'non-resident' landlords, it is 'usual place of abode' and not residency that determines whether a landlord is within the scheme or not.

An absence from the UK of six months or more determines that a person has a 'usual place of abode' outside of the UK. It is therefore possible for a person to be resident in the UK yet, for the purposes of the scheme, to have a 'usual place of abode' outside the UK.

Tax planning:

A 'non-resident individual' subject to income tax at the higher or additional rates might consider holding the property in a non-UK company.

Reasons:

An individual is taxed at the 40% or 45% income tax rates on the net rental profit whereas an overseas company pays corporation tax at 20% up to £300,000 net profit – the profit is likely to be much less than this amount.

Plus as the property is situated within the UK it will be subject to inheritance tax (IHT) if held by the individual as IHT is based on the location of assets. Companies are not subject to IHT.

However...such tax planning needs careful consideration as it was announced in the 2013 Budget that as from April 2013 not only will there be a levy where a company owns UK residential property valued at greater than £2m but also the capital gains tax (CGT) regime is to be extended to include the disposal of UK residential properties worth more than £2m by a non-resident, non-natural person or a disposal of shares or securities in a company holding such property by a non-resident person. This latter charge will not apply to genuine property businesses but will be charged on investment properties held within a company or trust.

53. NRLS – Agents

The 'Non-Resident Landlord Scheme' (NRLS) requires persons who act as 'representatives' (agents) for the landlord to deduct basic rate tax from the net rent collected (less expenses paid) unless the agent has authority from HMRC to pay the landlord gross.

The tax is paid on a quarterly basis and an information return is submitted. An annual return must also be submitted by 5 July after each tax year end and a certificate issued to the landlord confirming tax paid.

NRLS – Agents

John has been working abroad for eight months and rents out his UK property via a letting agent. The letting agent pays all expenses on his behalf, deducting them from the rent received. The property is let at £800 per month and the expenses are £250.

Amount of net rental profit John will receive is calculated:

£(800 – 250) x 80% = £440

The tax bill is £110 per month.

54.   NRLS – Repayments – Agents

Under the 'Non-Resident Landlord Scheme' (NRLS) where the deductible expenses exceed rental income for any quarter the excess expenses are:

- carried back for offset against rental income paid to the same landlord for previous quarters in the same tax year, on a 'last in, first out' basis; then
- carried forward for offset against future quarters' net rental profits.

Repayments

1. Carry back will result in a repayment of tax for the previous quarter in the tax year – the amount can be deducted from any tax due for other NRLS lettings of the current quarter.
2. Should it not be possible to deduct the refund because it relates to a previous tax year, a claim to HMRC is required.

NRLS – Repayments – Agents

John has been working abroad for nine months and rents out his UK property via a letting agent. The letting agent pays all the expenses on his behalf, deducting them from the rent received. The property is let at £800 per month. The expenses for the quarter to 31 March 2013 were £1,000 and for the quarter to 30 June 2013 were £1,400.

Tax year 2012/2013
Quarter to 30 December 2012
   Profit £800
   Tax   £160
Quarter to 31 March 2013
   Rent £800
   Less expenses £(1,000)
Carry back loss to previous quarter   £(200)
   Tax refund £200 @ 20%   £40

Tax year 2013/14
Quarter to 30 June 2013
   Rent   £800
   Less expenses   £(1,400)
   Excess expenses £(600)

The £(600) excess cannot be carried back to the previous quarter, as the quarter is not in the same tax year. Rather, it will be carried forward to be offset against future net profit (if the property remains rented). If the property ceases to be rented the excess cannot be used by the agent.

Note: The biggest expense is likely to be mortgage interest which is not paid by the agent and therefore cannot be offset. Hence many NRLS landlords have to wait until the year-end to claim any refund due via submission of a Tax Return.

55.   NRLS – Repayments – Tenants

The 'Non-Resident Landlords Scheme' (NRLS) requires that where there is no UK-based representative/agent, the rent being paid directly to a landlord who lives outside of the UK, the tenant must deduct basic rate tax from the rent paid and pay the tax to HMRC on a quarterly basis.

- The calculation is of tax on the gross amount actually payable to the landlord (plus any payments made by the tenant where the payment is not a deductible expense).
- Tenants do not have to operate the scheme if the rent paid is less than £5,200 per annum.
- Where the tenant occupies the property for only part of the year the amount of £5,200 is proportionately reduced.
- Where two or more people share a property as tenants the £5,200 limit applies separately to each in respect of each share of the rent.
- The tenant must make the tax payment plus submit an information return to HMRC confirming tax paid on a quarterly basis within 30 days of the end of each quarter (30 June, 30 September, 31 December and 31 March).
- By 5 July after the tax year end, the tenant must submit an annual return to HMRC and a certificate to the landlord confirming payments made.

Further details of the scheme can be found at: www.hmrc.gov.uk/cnr/nrl_guide_notes.pdf.

Chapter 8.
Selling Your Property

56.   Capital Gains Tax

Capital gains tax (CGT) is charged on the net gains (proceeds less cost) made on the sale of assets by individuals, personal representatives and trustees. Companies do not pay CGT – they are charged to corporation tax on net gains made.

Charge to CGT

A property investor is liable to CGT in the following circumstances:

- Where a property is sold at a higher price than the original purchase price.
- Where a property or part of a property is transferred to an individual who is not the transferor's spouse or civil partner.
- Individuals who are resident and domiciled in the UK are liable to CGT on assets sold wherever situated in the world.
- Non-domiciled persons are liable to CGT on UK assets and on gains brought into the country (known as the 'remittance basis').

Calculation of the tax

- Gains (or losses) are calculated separately for each asset.
- The net gains/losses for each property sold in a tax year are totalled and if the overall gain is greater than the annual exempt amount, the balance is taxed at the taxpayer's highest rate of tax applicable to capital gains – for individuals that is 18% for any amount falling in the basic rate band and 28% for any surplus. Companies have no annual exempt amount.
- A disposal may give rise to a gain or loss.
- The most common exempt asset is the main residence (the 'Principal Private Residence' - PPR).

57.   Consideration – 'Arm's Length' Rule

A property deal is termed as being made at 'arm's length' if it is a normal commercial transaction between two or more persons. A transaction not likely to be at arm's length is one undertaken by persons related by blood, adoption or marriage, or who are living together.

HMRC requires a valuation of property if the transaction has not been made at arm's length. The valuation will determine the market value and that will be used as the proceeds figure in the CGT calculation on sale.

Consideration – 'Arm's Length' Rule

Anton needed to sell his property quickly so that he could move abroad. Tony was aware that Anton needed a quick sale and therefore offered him a low price. No-one else made an offer. Anton accepted the offer.

This was not the best possible price that Anton could have achieved if he had left the property on the market for longer but he was trying to achieve the best deal possible. This is a bad bargain rather than being a bargain not made at arm's length and therefore the proceeds received will be used in any CGT calculation.

If Anton and Tony had been related (i.e. 'connected persons') HMRC would require a market valuation.

58. Valuing Land

A CGT charge may arise on the disposal of land. In order to calculate the capital gain or loss arising, a valuation is required where:

- the land was owned at 31 March 1982 (in order to determine the 'base cost' of the property);
- the disposal was a bargain not at 'arm's length';
- the disposal was to a connected person;
- there has already been a part disposal of some of the land and the 'alternative basis' of calculation has not been used.

Calculation

- 'Alternative' basis – the land disposed is treated as a separate asset – HMRC will accept any 'reasonable and fair' method of apportionment.
- Valuation – professional advice is required.

Valuing Land

Where a CGT computation requires a valuation HMRC offer a free valuation check. This service is available only after the disposal has been made but before completion of the Tax Return so you cannot ask for a check in advance of sale. Should HMRC's valuation differ from the taxpayer's valuation HMRC give alternatives and reasons.

59.   PPR Relief – Conditions

When an individual sells his only or main residence, generally the gain is exempt from CGT due to principal private residence (PPR) relief. However two conditions need to be fulfilled in that the property must:

- not have been purchased 'wholly or partly' for the reason of making a gain; and
- be the individual's only or main residence at some point of ownership.

The last 36 months of ownership of a property that has been the individual's only or main residence at some point is always treated as occupation for the purposes of the relief, regardless of whether the taxpayer is actually resident during those last 36 months.

PPR Relief – Conditions

Joan bought Rose Cottage on 1 June 2000, living there continuously until she inherited Brook House on 1 January 2003. She stayed at Brook House during the week as it was more convenient for her job, using Rose Cottage as a weekend retreat. Joan sold Rose Cottage on 1 June 2013.

Without a PPR election, Rose Cottage would be classed as Joan's PPR from 1 June 2000 to 31 December 2002 PLUS be allowed the 36 months from 2 June 2010 to the date of sale on 1 June 2013. Rose Cottage would not qualify for PPR relief for the period 1 January 2003 to 1 June 2010.

60.   Definition Of 'Residence'

One of the two main conditions to be fulfilled for PPR relief to apply is that the property must be the owner's only or main **'residence'** throughout the period of ownership.

Legislation does not define exactly what constitutes a 'residence' but in the tax case of *Batey v Wakefield* (1981) it was decided that not only can the main house comprise more than one building but also include ancillary buildings that are used as houses in their own right (e.g. summerhouse, staff bungalow).

Residence – Williams v Merrylees (1987)

A taxpayer purchased a small estate including a lodge sited approximately 200 metres from the main house. The lodge was occupied by a married couple who worked on the estate. The taxpayer sold the main house but retained the lodge after he moved.

When the occupants of the lodge died the taxpayer sold the lodge to the purchasers of the main house.

The commissioners found that the lodge was in the area of the main house and allowed the PPR relief claim.

61.   Choosing Your PPR – 'Flipping'

The owner of more than one residence can elect which residence to treat as the main PPR. The property does not need to be the main residence in practice, although he must have actually lived in the property as a residence at some time. The nominated property can be in the UK or abroad but there can only be one nominated PPR at any one time.

If the taxpayer fails to make an election HMRC will make the decision for them.

Choosing Your PPR – 'Flipping'

John has a house in Surrey that he purchased in April 2000 for £250,000. In April 2005 he purchased a flat in Hong Kong for £100,000. He immediately elects for the flat to be his PPR.

He sells the flat in August 2013 for £500,000 and as the property has been his PPR throughout the period of ownership the gain is fully tax free.

In the same month he sells his Surrey house making a capital gain of £150,000. On this property he is allowed to claim PPR for the period from April 2000 to April 2005 plus PPR for the last 36 months of ownership.

Had John not 'flipped' his main residence he would **not** have been entitled to PPR on the sale of the Hong Kong property and the gain of £400,000 would have been taxable.

62.   'Trigger' Events

As long as the initial election for PPR has been made, it can then be varied ('flipped') as many times as desired by submitting a further election. There is no prescribed form or wording for the election but it must be made within two years of a change in 'combination of residences'. If the two-year time limit is missed, there needs to be a 'trigger' event in order to reset the election date.

Examples of 'trigger' events that could be used to change the 'combination of residences' so that election is possible are:

- Marriage/civil partnership – both parties owning property used as their respective residence, or where there is joint ownership.
- Renting out one of the properties – when the letting comes to an end the owner can then take up residence.
- Selling half of one residence such that the seller is no longer in full ownership but is still in residence.
- Transferring ownership of a main residence into a trust under which the owner has a beneficial interest, with the proviso that the owner remains in residence. Care is needed so as not to be caught under the 'gift with reservation of benefit' or 'pre-owned asset' rules.

'Trigger' Events

John's main residence is in Woking; his father lives in Camberley. John's father dies and leaves his house to John, who lives in it at weekends. John is unaware of the election required and misses the election date. Three years after his father's death the election has still not been made. John marries Jane and the property is transferred into joint ownership. On marriage the election can be made.

63. Delay In Occupation

There is a limited concession to extend PPR relief should the owner not move into his only or main residence on purchase. This covers situations where the owner:

- buys land on which the house is to be built;
- has the house altered or decorated before moving in;
- remains in the first property whilst it is still on the market, provided that when that property is sold the second property becomes the owner's only or main residence.

In these circumstances, the period before occupation is allowed as PPR providing that the period between acquisition and actual occupation is 12 months or less. This period may be extended to a maximum of two years but only if HMRC is satisfied there is a good reason for the delay in occupation.

If the effect of this relief means that the owner temporarily has two PPR properties, an election is not required.

Delay in Occupation

Jim purchased 1 Back Lane on 1 January 1990 as his PPR. On 1 June 2007 he purchased 1 Front Lane intending to live there and rent Back Lane.

Unfortunately whilst undertaking some building work he discovered that Front Lane was deemed unsafe and returned to live in Back Lane whilst the repair work was being undertaken. The building work took 18 months; Jim moved into Front Lane which was eventually sold on 1 June 2012. PPR was granted for the full period of ownership.

64.   Deemed Occupation

There may be times when the owner is prevented from living in his main residence for reasons that are not his by choice. It would be unfair for him to not be eligible for PPR for that period of absence. 'Deemed' occupation is only possible where the taxpayer is absent from the property and he has no other residence eligible for PPR.

There is no minimum period of occupation for PPR relief but usually the house has to be physically occupied as a residence before and after any period of absence unless the reason for the absence was that the owner was working away, then he does not have to return to the house if his work subsequently requires residence elsewhere.

Three specific periods of absence qualify as 'deemed occupation':

1. Any period of absence – maximum three years.
2. Overseas employment (not self-employment) of himself or spouse/civil partner – unlimited period.
3. Employment elsewhere (employed or self-employed) of himself or spouse/civil partner – maximum four years.

Deemed Occupation

Stephen has a PPR property in Surrey but has worked in Wales for six years. His mother lives in Scotland and has recently become ill. Stephen intends to take unpaid leave from his job and be her carer.

He can do so for just one year to retain PPR on his Surrey property under the 'deemed occupation' rules. His six years working in Wales have used:

- Under point 3) – four years – employment elsewhere.

- Under point 1) – two years – any period.

- One year remains under point 1).

65.   Proving PPR Status (1)

PPR is a valuable tax relief and 'flipping' is legitimate tax planning. However, if used too many times or in quick succession, there is the danger that HMRC will investigate in an attempt to prove that either the PPR exemption is invalid and that the real reason for nominating the properties is avoidance of tax or that the owner should be taxed under the income tax rather than CGT rules as a 'serial seller'.

It is a matter of fact whether a property is the PPR or not but to allow a PPR claim HMRC require proof that the property has actually been lived in as the PPR.

Proving PPR – Status

In recent tax cases HMRC have tried to deny PPR using the following arguments:

- property utility bills not being in owner's name;
- other documentary evidence not showing the name and address (e.g. receipts for home or car insurance, telephone bills, DVLA records or credit reference agency records);
- property address not given as electoral register voting address;
- address not registered with a bank;
- neighbours not being aware of ownership;
- Tax Returns not giving PPR address.

66.   Proving PPR Status (2) – Intention

When deciding PPR status HMRC look for whether the owner had any **intention** of living in the property; they look for **'permanence, ...a degree of continuity and expectation of continuity to turn mere occupation into residence.'**   *Goodwin v Curtis* (1988).

Proving PPR Status – 'Intention'

Mr Metcalfe owned several properties but claimed one property as his PPR. The property was purchased 'off plan' and came with various fixtures and fittings (carpets, fridge, cooker, etc.).

As proof of non-permanence HMRC stated that no telephone had been installed but Mr Metcalfe argued that he always used his mobile; additional proof was required.

HMRC particularly cited the electricity bill showing low usage over the winter period suggesting non-residence. Mr Metcalfe argued that the bill was low because the apartment was new, had full double glazing and he worked long shifts.

He insisted that he had purchased the property with the **intention** of living there permanently but his work took him elsewhere. The Tribunal found that Mr Metcalfe had lived there for a time but could find no proof of *'permanence, continuity and expectation of continuity of occupation'* as the evidence was flimsy and more concrete evidence was lacking.

67. Conversion Of Property

Should a property that was initially a main residence be converted into flats and sold, PPR will be denied in respect of the gain attributable to the period of ownership whilst the conversion is taking place as the expenditure has been incurred wholly or partly for the purposes of realising a gain.

For the calculation a valuation of the property as not converted is required and then that figure is compared with the sale price post conversion in order to establish the additional profit attributable to the conversion.

Conversion of Property

Tony lived in a property as his main residence from the date of purchase in July 1996 (cost = £100,000) to July 2011 when work commenced on conversion into three flats. Work was completed in December 2011, the flats finally all being sold in June 2013 for £250,000 each.

The conversion cost was £150,000. If the property had remained as one house the sale proceeds would have been £550,000.

The additional expenditure for conversion generated an additional gain of £50,000 calculated as follows:

	Total Gain	Exempt PPR Gain	Taxable Gain
Proceeds/valuation	£750,000	£550,000	£200,000
Original cost of property	£(100,000)	£(100,000)	
Conversion expenditure	£(150,000)		£(150,000)
Gain	£500,000	£450,000	£50,000

68. PPR and Dependent Relative Relief

PPR relief is not allowed on the sale of property purchased as the residence of an elderly or infirm ('dependent') relative.

However, PPR is allowed on property that was used by the relative prior to 5 April 1988, providing that the relative was the property's sole resident, living there rent-free and continued to do so until three years before sale.

If there had been a change of occupant after 5 April 1988 the exemption is not allowed for the period after the change to the date of sale even if the new occupant is another dependent relative. 'Dependent relative' is defined as being the owner's own or their spouse/civil partner's widowed or separated mother or any other relative who is unable to look after themselves.

PPR and Dependent Relative Relief

David acquired a property on 1 June 1985 and sold it on 1 December 2013 realising a gain of £250,000. The house was provided rent-free and without any other consideration as the sole residence of David's widowed mother from 1 June 1985 to 1 December 1989 when she died. David's elderly mother-in-law then took up residence.

1 June 1985 – 1 December 2013 = 342 months

sole residence of dependent relative:
1 June 1985 – 1 December 1989 = 54 months

final period (last 3 years exempt) = 36 months

PPR relief allowed:

<u>54 months + 36 months</u> x £250,000 = <u>£65,789</u>
  342 months

Chargeable gain is £250,000 less PPR of £65,789 = £184,211.

69. Job-Related Accommodation

If a taxpayer owns a property as his main residence but is obliged to live elsewhere in job-related accommodation, the property could be deemed not eligible for PPR relief. However, PPR relief will apply when, during the period of ownership:

- he resides in other job-related accommodation; *and*
- he intends to occupy the first property as his only or main residence at some time.

This 'job-related' provision is only possible if it is necessary or customary for the employee to live in accommodation provided by the employer for the better performance of their duties – it must not simply be a matter of choice. The relief is allowed even if the first property is not occupied due to a change of circumstances, provided it has been the *intention* to occupy the property.

Job-Related Accommodation

Susan occupied her main residence until 2000 when her work required her to move into qualifying job-related accommodation in Scotland. In 2005 she was sent to work in the Devon office but occupied privately rented accommodation. She purchased that property in 2007.

In 2013 the original residence was sold, not having been re-occupied. Until 2007 she had intended to return to her main residence.

PPR relief is allowed:

- until 2000 before the move to Scotland;
- for the period of job-related accommodation between 2000 to 2005; and
- for the final 36 months.

70. Selling Sequence

There is a restriction on the size of garden or grounds attached to a main residence that can be granted PPR relief. The 'permitted area' must not exceed half a hectare (approximately 1.25 acres); this area is the total area, including the grounds on which the residence is built.

However, a larger area may be permitted should it prove to be needed for the 'reasonable enjoyment' of the house as a residence, commensurate with the size and character of the property.

Care must be taken as to the order of sale – if the property is sold before the land then CGT will be charged as the land will no longer be 'attached' to the residence. If PPR is claimed HMRC will want to know what has changed such that land necessary for the 'reasonable enjoyment' of the house before sale was not so required afterwards.

Selling Sequence

Mr Varty purchased a house comprising land of less than one acre. He sold the house with part of the garden and applied for planning permission for the remainder which was sold four years later. HMRC charged CGT on the second sale and the taxpayer appealed, contending that the land had been 'enjoyed' as part of his main residence and that the gain was PPR exempt.

It was held that PPR did not apply. Tax case - *Varty v Lynes* (1976).

71.   Lodgers

HMRC will allow the letting of **one lodger** in a main residence without the PPR exemption being affected.

However, this is on the proviso that the lodger is treated as a member of the family such that they are at least allowed to share living rooms and take meals with the family.

The PPR exemption will be denied should there be **more than one lodger** and in this instance the 'letting relief' exemption will be relevant.

Lodgers

Some owners could be tempted not to declare the presence of a lodger on their income Tax Return, particularly if the rental income is under the 'rent-a-room' relief limit.

However, they should do so as this will notify HMRC that letting relief is to be a factor on any subsequent sale.

72. Working From Home

PPR is not available in respect of any part of the main residence that is used **exclusively** for business use.

To protect the exemption, any part of the home that is used for business purposes needs to also be available for private use. For example, a room used as an office from which to run the business during the day could also be used by the taxpayer's children to do their homework in the evening.

Where there is exclusive business use, any gain arising on sale must be apportioned and the proportion relating to exclusive business use will be charged to CGT. However, the gain relating to the use of one room may be below the annual exempt amount and not be charged.

Working from Home

Julia runs a marketing business from home. Her home has eight rooms and she uses one exclusively as an office. On the sale of her property, she realises a gain of £50,000. One eighth (£6,250) would be charged to CGT. To the extent that her annual exemption (£10,900 for the tax year 2013/2014) remains available, this would shelter the gain with the result that no CGT is payable.

73.   Lettings Relief

A property that is rented qualifies for 'residential lettings exemption' ('lettings relief') on sale but only if the residence has been the owner's main residence (or elected to be so) at any time in his period of ownership.

The exemption is restricted to the smallest of £40,000, the amount attributable to the period for which the property was let and the amount equal to the exempt gain on the proportion of the property that had been occupied by the owner.

The relief is per person, therefore a property owned jointly is allowed maximum relief of £80,000.

It has not been confirmed via a court case but there seems to be no reason why a property let under the 'furnished holiday lettings' rules should not be eligible to claim 'lettings relief' so long as the property has been the owner's main residence at some time during the period of ownership.

Lettings Relief

Holly owned a property that was part main residence and part let. The gain on sale was £80,000. It was agreed with HMRC that the proportion of gain relating to the let part was £48,000 – the balance of £32,000 related to the main residence and was therefore PPR exempt.

The £48,000 gain on the let part is reduced by the lowest of:

1. £48,000 (the amount attributable to the let part)

2. £40,000; and

3. £32,000 (the amount equal to the exempt PPR gain).

Thus a total of £64,000 is exempt (i.e. £32,000(point 3) + £32,000(PPR)).

Amount chargeable to tax: £80,000 – £64,000 = £16,000

Less annual exemption if not already used.

74.   Surrender Premiums

A premium is a sum paid by a tenant to a landlord either on the creation or surrender of an interest in a property.

Surrender premiums payable to terminate a lease early are generally tax inefficient; depending on the length of the lease and whether or not there is a provision in the agreement for early termination, the landlord will be taxed on a capital and/or revenue receipt whilst the tenant receives neither a capital nor revenue deduction.

Tax planning possibilities:

- Rather than pay the premium the tenant incentivises a third party (new tenant) to accept assignment of the lease. The payment is tax free in the new tenant's hands and he may be willing to accept a lower incentive from the existing tenant as a share of the tax saving from which he will benefit. The agreement must be made directly between the existing and new tenant without any input from the landlord.
- The tenant offers the landlord a sum representing the future rent due with an appropriate discount to represent the cash-flow benefit to the landlord. The tenant then sub-lets to the landlord for the remainder of the lease period at a peppercorn rent, thus enabling the landlord to not lose out financially compared with an outright surrender, the tenant will be able to claim a tax deduction for the sum paid. If that amount is close to the original premium, the tax relief improves the tenant's position. The landlord would have to consider his position as the receipt will be of income and not capital.

75. Entrepreneurs' Relief

Entrepreneurs' relief can only be claimed by individuals; it cannot be claimed by companies.

It is available on a capital gain arising on the disposal of a business asset which is linked to, or takes place as part of, a disposal of all or part of a business. For these purposes a 'business' is a trade, profession or vocation.

Thus, the relief is not generally available on disposals of residential property but is allowed on the sale of furnished holiday lets (as the properties are regarded as business assets) or potentially on the disposal of a property that has been used as a home and business premises, in which case the property must be sold no later than three years after the business.

The effect of the relief is to reduce the CGT rate charged from 28% or 18% to 10%.

Entrepreneurs' Relief

Mr Jones, a dentist, runs his practice from a surgery attached to his home which is calculated as 25% of the property area. He is disposing of his home and business on retirement. The gain on disposal is £800,000 and the goodwill is £400,000. The tax liability will be:

Gain on home 25% x £800,000	£200,000
Gain on Goodwill	£400,000
Total Gain	£600,000
Less Annual Exemption 2013/2014	£(10,900)
Chargeable Gain	£589,100
Tax liability @ 10%	£58,910

Chapter 9.
Gifting Your Property

76. Gift To Spouse/Civil Partner

If a gift of a property (or share of a property) is made or a property is sold at less than its market value, CGT is charged as if the donor had received the market value in cash.

This ruling does not apply to transfers (gifts) between spouses/civil partnerships. In this situation the donee is treated as having acquired the property at the date of the transaction but most importantly at the original purchase price. No CGT will be due until the receiving spouse/civil partner sells the property.

Gift To Spouse

Joe is a 45% additional rate taxpayer who owns a BTL property originally purchased for £150,000. He gifts it to his son on 1 May 2013 when its value is £250,000. Joe is deemed to have received the market value and as such his CGT tax liability is:

Market value less original price	£100,000
Less Annual Exemption 2013/2014	£(10,900)
Chargeable Gain	£89,100
Tax liability @ 28%	£24,948

However, there will be a practical problem in that no monies will have been received out of which to pay the CGT.

If Joe had gifted the property to his wife no CGT would be due on transfer but should his wife subsequently sell the property, the base value would be the original cost of £150,000.

77.   Gift Of PPR To Spouse/Civil Partner

Where there is an inter-spouse/civil partner transfer of a Principal Private Residence (PPR), the donee is still treated as having acquired the property at the donor's base cost but with one added twist – the donee's period of ownership is deemed to commence not at the date of transfer but instead at the date of the original acquisition by the donor.

Furthermore, any period during which the property was the main residence of the donor will also be deemed to be that of the donee such that the transaction is back dated.

This is only relevant to properties that are (or have been nominated as) the main PPR.

Gift Of PPR To Spouse

Joe purchases property 1 in his sole name as a main residence. A few years later he marries Jane, moves into property 2 and lets out property 1. 10 years later there is a large capital gain accruing on property 1.

Joe then transfers property 1 to Jane on a 'no gain/no loss' basis and they start also to occupy property 1 as a residence.

Jane elects property 1 as the main PPR. A few weeks later a further election is made back to property 2. Over the next few months Joe and Jane live in property 1 as a residence before the property is sold.

Under this specific ruling property 1 is deemed to be the main PPR for the period from the date of purchase to the date of transfer; then as the property has been a residence, the period between the date of transfer and the date of sale is also CGT-free as it is covered by the three-year rule.

78. Exchange Of Interests

If a gift of property is made to a non-spouse/civil partner, CGT is charged on the donor as if the market value had actually been received.

However, in a situation where joint owners of property wish to become sole owners of part, then provided no money changes hands, a form of 'reinvestment relief' can be applied and no CGT charged.

The joint owners are treated as if each had sold their share for its market value and then the proceeds 'reinvested' in acquiring the other's half share.

If the properties are not of equal value or if one of the joint owners pays extra for a higher percentage share, CGT will be charged on the person receiving payment equivalent to the actual amount paid.

Exchange Of Interests

Alan and Brian (who are not connected persons) jointly own two rental properties, Greengables and Whitegables, respectively. Each property was originally inherited at market values of £50,000 each. They decide to exchange their joint interests such that Alan acquires the sole interest in Greengables and Brian secures exclusive title to Whitegables. At the time of exchange Greengables has a market value of £200,000; Whitegables a value of £250,000. No cash changes hands but Brian has obtained the more valuable interest and therefore greater consideration.

Cost for future CGT purposes = Cost of original ½ share + deemed cost of ½ share in exchange.

Alan's calculation:

MV consideration	£100,000
Less cost	£(25,000)
Less 'reinvestment'	£(75,000)
Gain	NIL

Brian's calculation:

MV consideration	£125,000
Less cost	£(25,000)
Less 'reinvestment'	£(75,000)
Chargeable Gain on exchange	£ 25,000

Cost for future CGT purposes for both properties:
£25,000 + £25,000 = £50,000

79. Exchange Of Interests – Main Residence Problem

A form of 'reinvestment relief' is available in situations where ownership of property is swapped or is changed from joint ownership to each owning their specific part.

A significant exception to this relief is if any of the properties is, or has at any time been, a Principal Private Residence (PPR) of one of the owners or later becomes their PPR, such that a disposal within the next six years following exchange is eligible for PPR relief to any extent.

However, if **all** of the properties involved in the exchange become solely owned PPRs of their respective individual owners then the reinvestment relief may still apply. (Married couples count as 'sole' owners in this context.)

The 'main residence problem' is that this 'exception to the exception' only applies if **all parties'** properties are their respective main PPR.

Exchange Of Interests – Main Residence Problem

Susan and Sharon jointly own two cottages, each living in one as their main PPR. They exchange interests such that Susan's house becomes the PPR of Sharon and vice versa. As no money has changed hands, the 'reinvestment relief' will apply and no CGT will be charged.

However, if Susan had lived in her cottage as her main PPR but Sharon's main PPR was another property, the 'relief' would not be available.

80.   'Value Shifting'

'Value shifting' occurs when the value of a property is altered as a result of passing an interest in the property to another.

Anti-avoidance rules are in place whereby such disposals are deemed to be chargeable to CGT despite there being no consideration involved. In these situations the 'market value' rule is deemed to operate and the person transferring the value is liable to CGT based on the amount which he or she could have obtained for the transfer, if the parties had been at arm's length.

The main instance where these anti-avoidance rules operate are in the situation where the owner of a freehold property effectively changes the type of ownership by disposing of the freehold while granting a leasehold to himself, thereby reducing the value of the property. Any subsequent alteration to the lease will automatically result in a CGT charge despite no consideration having been received.

'Value Shifting'

Mr James owns a commercial property currently valued at £200,000 with an original purchase price of £120,000. If he gifts the property to his son, with no consideration, the transaction would be treated as if he had sold at the 'market value' as the two are 'connected persons'. So he gives the freehold to his son, granting himself a lease for 99 years at a rent of £1 per year. The value of the freehold will be negligible.

He then arranges for the lease to be altered so that the rent is at the market rate resulting in the increase in value of the freehold. The change in the terms of the lease is an example of 'value shifting' because the lease itself has become less valuable but the freehold more valuable.

At the date of alteration of the lease Mr James will be charged to CGT on the basis that he has disposed of an asset equal to the value transferred. If the value of the £1 per year lease was £200,000 and the 'market value' lease £60,000, the value transferred would be £140,000.

The corresponding deductible cost is calculated in proportion to the value deemed to be transferred (£140,000), against the original value (£200,000).

$$\frac{£140,000}{£200,000} \times £120,000 = £84,000$$

Capital Gain calculation:

Deemed Proceeds	£140,000
Less value transferred	£(84,000)
Chargeable Gain	£ 56,000

81.   'Hold-Over' Relief

'Hold-over' relief is a way of deferring payment of CGT on certain assets including land and buildings used in a business until the new owner of the asset sells. The donee, in effect, takes over the original cost of the asset and may eventually have to pay CGT on both the gain incurred from the date of gift plus the gain 'held over'.

HMRC have produced Help Sheet 295 *'Relief of gifts and similar transactions'* that details the procedure. A claim form needs to be signed and submitted.

'Hold-Over' Relief

Judy owns a second home which shows a significant gain. She gives the cottage to her husband Jim. This is treated as a 'no gain/no loss' disposal between them as they are married. Jim is treated as acquiring the cottage for the price that Judy paid originally (so preserving the gain in his hands), as from the date of the inter-spouse disposal.

Jim manages the property as a qualifying furnished holiday let and after a year gives the property to their adult daughter, Louise, claiming hold-over relief so that Louise takes over her mother's historic base cost.

Louise occupies the property as her only or main residence. When the property is sold full PPR relief will be allowed.

82. Gifting To Charity

Relief from income tax, capital gains tax and inheritance tax is possible should a property be gifted to a charity or sold to a charity at less than the market value. The donor must gift the entire property. He cannot derive any benefit; neither can he continue to live at the property. Where property is owned jointly, relief is only available if the entire property is gifted and at least one owner must be an individual.

Income tax relief

Relief is at market value plus associated costs less any money or benefit received in return.

Capital gains tax relief

The disposal is treated as being a 'no gain, no loss' disposal, therefore no tax is charged. If the property is sold for less than market value but for more than cost a capital gain will arise on the difference.

Inheritance tax relief

The value of a gift to charity is deducted from the value of the estate if left in a will.

Gifting To Charity

Ron is a 45% additional rate taxpayer who in May 2013 donated a property valued at £150,000 to a charity. Legal fees on transfer amounted to £1,200. In return the charity gives him the benefit of tickets to attend their main fund-raising event valued at £300.

Tax relief : £150,000 + (£1,200 – £300) = £150,900 @ 45% = £67,905

Chapter 10.
Minimising Inheritance Tax And The Use Of Trusts

83. Lifetime Planning – Property

Inheritance tax (IHT) is charged on the value (assets less liabilities) of a person's estate on death. The first £325,000 is exempt (the 'nil rate band') and the balance is taxed at 40%.

Inheritance tax planning – property

- Transfers between spouses/civil partners are exempt from IHT, therefore, if property is left to the surviving spouse/civil partner there will be no IHT due on the first death but may be on the second death.
- If a gift of property is made to someone who is not married or in a civil partnership with the donor, the transfer is termed a 'potentially exempt' transfer and will only be chargeable to IHT should the donor not survive seven years. This exemption will not apply if the property gifted has conditions attached (termed a 'gift with reservation of benefit'- see Tip 84) or was originally the donor's property ('pre-owned asset'- see Tip 85).
- Property placed within a 'Mainstream' trust does not form part of the donor's estate on death and as such reduces any IHT that may become due.

84.   Gift With Reservation Of Benefit

The ideal in IHT lifetime planning would be to gift the main residence out of the estate but at the same time remain living there. However, the **'gift with reservation of benefit'** (GWRB) rules do not allow a simple transfer of a whole or even part of a property to another whilst the donor remains in residence (i.e. 'reserves a benefit'). Should such a transaction take place the property is treated as remaining within the donor's estate on death.

In order for the disposal to not be deemed a 'gift' for IHT purposes there needs to be a sale at full market value.

Gift With Reservation of Benefit

In 2008 James sold a house then worth £100,000 to his adult son for £25,000. James remained in the house until he died in 2013. The disposal is a GWRB and the value of the property gifted was 75% of the total value.

Thus, 75% of the property's value at death is treated as James' property and the value will be liable to IHT.

85.   Pre-Owned Asset Tax

The '**pre-owned assets tax**' (POAT) is an income tax charge levied on the 'benefit' earned on any property that had been formerly owned by the user (or for which he has provided funds to purchase), but of which he still enjoys the use, unless sold to an unconnected person in a bargain at arm's length.

The benefit is calculated by reference to the rental value of the property. This is the rent that would have been payable if it had been let to the taxpayer at an annual open market rent.

There are exemptions to the charge and a 'de minimis' amount (£5,000 per tax year per spouse/civil partner), but it is not possible to transfer any unused exemption from one to the other.

Note:

- Either GWRB or the POAT rules could apply in the situation where a donor has gifted the property, remaining in residence but paying no or minimal rent.
- If POAT applies and it is not viable to meet the tax bill but there is less concern about the IHT bill, an election can be made for the GWRB rules to apply instead of the POAT.

Pre-Owned Asset Tax

In 2008 James gave his son £250,000 which he spends on acquiring Greenacres. James moves into the property on 6 April 2013; he will be subject to the POAT charge as from that date. If the market rent of the property is £5,000 and no rent is paid then there will be no POAT charge. If the market rent is £10,000 and James pays a rent of £5,000, the full £10,000 will be subject to the POAT charge.

Note: if James had moved into a house that Jim had bought with his own money and then James gave him funds which were used for improvements, then there will be no POAT charge; this is because James' money has not been used to acquire an interest in the property. Likewise if there is a gap of at least seven years since an outright gift of money, the resulting asset is not 'traced back' to the gift/donor.

86. Lifetime Planning – Selling The Main Residence

Suggestions

- Sell the property, downsize and make a cash gift to a donee out of the proceeds. The amount of gift needs to be sufficient to reduce the taxable estate to below the exempt amount, the remaining money being used to purchase a smaller, less costly property. The gift of cash is a deemed potentially exempt transfer (PET) for IHT purposes and there will be no gift with reservation of benefit problems as there is no retained benefit. However, the donor does have to live for seven years for the gift to be totally IHT-free.

- Sell the property to a donee for the market price and then lease the property back, paying the full market rent to live there. The monies received could then be gifted in the form of PETs, or spent. Any capital appreciation will accrue to the recipient, the purchase money being raised via a qualifying loan. There would be practical issues such as the seller's security of tenure, stamp duty land tax payable on the sale, the market rent would be subject to income tax in the recipient's hands, and the CGT PPR would possibly not be available for the recipient on the subsequent sale of the property.

87.   Lifetime Planning – Gifting The Main Residence

Suggestions

- Gift the property and then pay full market rent to live there. The gift will be a potentially exempt transfer (PET) for IHT purposes; income tax on the rent will be paid by the donee.

- Mortgage the house, giving away the proceeds or invest the money in assets that potentially do not attract IHT, for example AIM shares. After two years, the investments will qualify for 100% relief from IHT and the mortgage will reduce the value of the house for IHT purposes. However, mortgage interest will be charged. The funds borrowed could be gifted as a PET.

- Move to a rented property and give the main residence away. The gift will be a PET. If the gift is made within three years of the date of moving no CGT will be charged if the property has been the individual's only or main residence throughout the period of ownership.

88. Lifetime Planning – Retaining The Main Residence

The only IHT planning scheme in relation to the main residence that HMRC accept as valid is a co-ownership arrangement where, for example, parents and adult children live together in one property.

The parents put the property into the joint names of themselves and their adult children under a co-ownership arrangement as 'tenants in common'. This type of arrangement is not caught by the 'gift with reservation of benefit' (see Tip 84) or 'pre-owned asset' (see Tip 85) tax rules.

The only area of dispute with this arrangement is as to whether the co-ownership must be equal between all parties, or whether it is possible to retain only a small interest and for each adult child to have a substantially greater interest than is retained by the parents.

89.   IHT Planning – Use Of Trusts

What is a trust?

A trust is created when a person (a 'settlor') transfers assets to people whom they 'trust' ('trustees') to hold them on behalf of others ('beneficiaries').

Why use a trust?

- *Convenience* – the beneficiary may be a minor who is unable, as yet, to take responsibility for the property themselves, or the settlor may be looking for flexibility to provide for a class of beneficiaries who might not even be born at the time the trust is created (such as grandchildren).
- *Reduce taxation* – property placed within a 'Mainstream' trust does not form part of the settlor's estate on death and as such reduces any inheritance tax that may be due; and for the main reason to...
- *Protect the property* — in case:

  - the beneficiary turns out to be someone who cannot manage the property themselves, or
  - the property would otherwise need to be sold to pay for long-term care, or
  - to protect the property from potential bankruptcy or divorce.

Different types of trust for properties

1. Qualifying 'Interest in Possession' (QIIP) trusts; and
2. 'Mainstream' trusts (also termed 'discretionary' trusts) being:

   - 'Nil rate band' trusts.
   - 'Charge' trusts.

Under a QIIP trust, a beneficiary is entitled to the income as well as the underlying property held within the trust whereas with a 'Mainstream' trust no one is entitled to either the income or property; rather it is at the *discretion* of the trustees as to how both are distributed dependent upon the terms of the Trust Deed.

Trust planning is for the long term and can be used to secure assets, including property, which are likely to grow in value.

90.   'Interest In Possession' Trust

How does it work?

- The beneficiary has the right to receive an income for a defined period (usually for the remainder of the beneficiary's life) but not the right to the capital held within the trust. Thus, rented property can produce the income but the property itself remains within the trust.

- The 'interest' will cease when the beneficiary becomes *'absolutely entitled'* to the trust assets either on death or when some special condition is met (e.g. upon reaching a specified age, say, 18 years). On being absolutely entitled the beneficiary can direct the trustees as to how to deal with the property; he may even require the property to be transferred to him.

Advantages

- 'Interest in possession' trusts are a potentially useful way of providing a safe income for dependants of the settlor, whilst ensuring that the property is saved to be passed on at a later date.

- On the death of someone who has an 'interest in possession', the 'interest' comes to an end and the beneficiary becomes absolutely entitled to the trust property but no CGT is due (but neither are any capital losses allowable).

- A chargeable gain will only arise to the trust if the cost of the property had been reduced by 'hold-over' relief on transfer into the trust. The gain being equal to the amount 'held over'.

91. 'Nil Rate Band' Trust

How does it work?

- A 'nil rate band' (NRB) 'Mainstream' trust is created on death in a sum to include property equal in value to the inheritance tax NRB (currently £325,000) or the settlor's unused NRB if already part-used.
- Each spouse/civil partner must own the property as 'tenants in common'.
- The surviving spouse has the legal right to occupy the property by virtue of ownership of their own half-share.
- The trustees are deemed to own a beneficial 50% share of the property which is effectively subject to a sitting tenant; the property cannot be sold because they do not entirely own it.

Advantages

- Maximum flexibility over the estate; spouse IHT exemption retained.
- No problems should a beneficiary become bankrupt or die.
- Principal Private Residence Relief is available on the whole value of the property if sold.
- The remaining estate assets can be left outright.
- Assets held in trust are not assessed as capital of the surviving spouse for long-term care.
- Guarantee that the trust assets pass per the donor's wishes.

92. 'Charge' Trust

How does it work?

- On the first death property is transferred into a 'Mainstream' trust with the gain made on transfer being 'held over'.
- Trustees are given the power to accept a loan note/charge/IOU. The loan is kept by the trustees as a debt of the estate until 'called in' on the death of the second spouse.
- The surviving spouse will normally have no personal liability for the charge which can be index-linked to take into account future increases in the IHT nil rate band (NRB).
- Alternatively, the charge can be expressed as a proportion of the value of the property calculated periodically thereby benefiting from any capital appreciation, or it could be made to track a publicly available index of property prices for comparable properties.
- On the second death the loan to the trust is repaid out of the estate. The NRB is applied to the remainder of the estate assets.

Advantages

- The property remains owned by the surviving spouse and benefits from either the PPR should the property be subsequently sold or a base cost uplift if retained until death.
- On the death of the surviving spouse IHT will be payable but reduced by the charge and, if calculated correctly, to below the NRB.
- Should the property be a residential let the trustees are allowed to offset the interest paid against the rental income received.

93. CGT 'Hold-Over' Relief And Trusts

On the transfer of property into a trust, the original owner of the property (the 'settlor') is treated as having gifted the property to the trust at market value for capital gains tax (CGT) purposes. The 'market value' rule applies because the settlor and trust are deemed to be 'connected' when the trust comes into existence.

If the property transferred has increased in value since the date of acquisition, then the settlor will have a chargeable gain and possibly CGT to pay. However, the settlor can claim to defer ('hold over') the charge if the trust has been created whilst the settlor is alive (assets transferred into a trust on death do not attract CGT).

'Hold-over' relief is a way to defer paying CGT until the trust sells the property. The relief is not available should the settlor retain an interest in the property transferred.

CGT 'Hold-Over' Relief And Trusts

Andy creates a trust whilst he is still alive and transfers two properties into it. The original total purchase price of the properties was £300,000; the value at the date of transfer into the trust is £500,000 – the gain of £200,000 being 'held over'.

Four years later the trust sells the properties for £1,000,000. The trust will be liable to tax on a total gain of £700,000 – comprising the gain made whilst the properties were held within the trust and the gain 'held over'.

94. CGT 'Hold-Over' Relief, Trusts And PPR Problem

The beneficiary of a trust can live in a property held within a trust as their main residence and on the future disposal of the property Principal Private Residence (PPR) relief will be available.

However, if a 'hold-over' election was made on transfer into the trust PPR is denied on any subsequent sale. This is the position whether the trust sells the property or the property is transferred out of the trust and then the transferee sells.

So the choice is between:

1. paying CGT at the date of transfer into the trust based on the market value and claiming PPR relief on the future sale; or
2. 'holding over' the gain on transfer into the trust but the trust being liable to CGT on the whole gain on the final sale.

CGT 'Hold-Over' Relief, Trusts And PPR Problem

Where a property has been subject to a 'hold over' relief election, PPR exemption is no longer available until after it has been sold to a third party.

Consider not electing for 'hold over' relief into the trust but opting to pay CGT sooner rather than later, especially if it is thought that CGT rates are likely to rise in the future.

95. 'Mesher' Order Trusts

A '**Mesher**' **order** is a court order that postpones the sale of the marital home, the actual date of sale being dependent upon certain specified events.

If the property subject to the order is sold more than three years after the date of separation then the calculation is the proportion of gain made after the three years in relation to the total period of ownership or 31 March 1982, whichever is the latest date. The only situation where HMRC will allow more than three years' absence is when the property is transferred to the spouse/or civil partner as part of a 'Mesher' order and a PPR election has not been made.

HMRC view a 'Mesher' order as creating a trust for CGT purposes and as such the settlor party is treated as having transferred the property into the trust at market value even though the party transferring the property retains an interest. The market value applies because the settlor and trust are deemed to be 'connected'.

The property will be deemed 'relevant property' for IHT purposes and as such liable to the ten-yearly and exit charges. This may present difficulties as the trust will not normally have liquid funds to meet the charges. These charges are currently at a maximum of 6%.

'Mesher' Order Trusts

An alternative to a 'Mesher' order is for the non-occupying party to place a charge over the property for a fixed sum with interest on the basis that the property be transferred to the occupying party subject to that charge. CGT will not apply on sale as such a charge does not constitute an interest in the property.

96.   Sales After Death

Beneficiaries under a deceased's will are deemed to inherit the assets at their market value at the date of death. However, if a property is sold within four years of death at a lower price than the value used for the inheritance tax (IHT) calculation on the estate, that earlier IHT liability can be reduced by substituting the lower sale proceeds for the agreed value, therefore saving the estate IHT.

The relief is known as 'loss on sale of land relief' and if there is more than one property sold in the four years after death, the sale price of all those sold must be substituted for the values at death.

This relief is not available where:

- the difference between the date of death value and the sale price is less than £1,000 or 5% of the value on death, whichever is the lower; or
- the sale is to the spouse/civil partner, children or remoter descendant or trustees.

Sales After Death

Molly died in September 2010 owning a property valued for IHT purposes at £400,000. The property was eventually sold for £360,000 in 2013.

The loss on the probate value is: £400,000 – £360,000 = £(40,000).

Depending upon the value of the estate, up to £16,000 inheritance tax can be refunded.

Calculation: £40,000 x 40% = £16,000.

97. Furnished Holiday Lets – Business Property Relief

For income tax and capital gains tax purposes the operation of a furnished holiday let (FHL) is treated as a business. However, a recent tax case has confirmed that a FHL is not automatically to be treated as a business for inheritance tax purposes and as such business property relief (BPR) may not be allowed.

BPR provides relief from IHT on the transfer of a business or interest in a business asset at a rate of 100%. For BPR to apply the business must be carried on with the view of making a profit and be run on sound business principles.

However, in the BPR relief case of *HMRC v Pawson* (2013) it was decided that a FHL would not normally qualify for BPR and that only where the level of 'services' provided to the holidaymaker is significant would BPR be granted.

This decision brings matters much more into line with other BPR cases and although it should not preclude *all* furnished holiday lets from qualifying for BPR it will be more difficult to obtain; as ever each case will depend on its own facts.

Furnished Holiday Lets – Business Property Relief

NOTE: in Tip 97 of the first edition of '101 Property Tax Secrets Revealed' it was stated that a FHL WOULD be treated as a business and as such a BPR claim would be possible.

That was the ruling at the time of writing but since the publication of that book the *Pawson* case was being heard by a higher court and it was then decided that a FHL is not a business for IHT purposes.

Chapter 11.
Minimising Stamp Duty Land Tax

98.   Multiple Dwellings Relief

Stamp duty land tax (SDLT) is charged whenever a transaction involving land takes place, however effected. It is levied as a percentage of the amount paid where the amount is above a certain threshold. It is a 'stepped' tax: the rate increases on the whole of the purchase price at certain thresholds.

Multiple dwellings relief allows a rate to be charged at the percentage payable on the 'average property' price should more than one property be purchased at one time, rather than on the total consideration.

Note: the minimum rate charged is 1%; therefore it is not beneficial to claim this relief for properties valued at under £250,000 – the usual SDLT rate limit.

Multiple Dwellings Relief

Ben wants to buy flats being offered at a significant discount for bulk purchase. Four flats will cost £200,000 each plus a penthouse flat at £300,000.

Without claiming multiple dwellings relief the SDLT charge would be 5% on the full purchase price of £1.1m, i.e. £55,000.

With claiming the relief he pays 1% on the total consideration as the average price is £220,000 – only £11,000, resulting in a tax saving of £44,000.

99.   Gifting Property

Stamp duty land tax (SDLT) is charged on *'money or money's worth',* defined very widely to include consideration given directly by the purchaser or person connected with the purchaser.

Consideration is the purchase price plus any additional amounts paid in the transaction (e.g. seller's fees).

Cash is obviously the commonest form of consideration on a sale but as a general rule the market value is used when gifted unless:

- the property is gifted subject to a mortgage when the donee is deemed to take over the donor's share of the mortgage and SDLT is charged on that amount; or
- the transfer is of connected property.

Gifting Property

Anne owns a BTL property worth £500,000 on which there is a mortgage of £350,000. Anne transfers the property from sole into joint names with her husband Adrian. There is no CGT because gifts between spouses are CGT-free.

Adrian will take over half of the mortgage and be deemed to have 'paid' that amount for his half share of the property. SDLT will be payable of £1,750 (£175,000 x 1%).

100. Transfer Of Connected Property

If property transactions are linked (which would be the situation on a sale between 'connected' persons), HMRC do not look at each transaction in isolation in order to determine the rate of SDLT to charge, rather the proceeds are aggregated.

Transfer of Connected Property

John purchases a BTL property for £300,000 – the SDLT will be £9,000 (3% rate). If the seller does a deal whereby the house is sold to John for £250,000 and the garden is sold to John's wife in a separate transaction for £50,000 you might assume that the SDLT liability would amount to £2,500 on John's property (1% rate) and the garden not be taxed as being under the £125,000 0% rate limit.

However, HMRC link the two transactions together as the two purchasers are 'connected' and SDLT of £9,000 will be payable.

101. Tax Evasion v Tax Avoidance

Tax evasion is the deliberate escaping from paying tax that should be paid and usually entails taxpayers deliberately misrepresenting or concealing the true state of their affairs to the tax authorities.

The Government has invested over £900m in putting procedures in place in order to identify tax evasion. Such procedures include the publishing of a 'FBI-style' list of 'mugshots' of people who are *'tax criminals who have absconded after being charged with a crime or during trial'*.

Tax avoidance is the exploitation of rules in order to reduce the tax that would otherwise be paid.

HMRC have developed the **Tax Avoidance Disclosure** rules, under which certain tax planning schemes must be notified to HMRC shortly after they are marketed or implemented. HMRC then consider the scheme and decide whether the scheme is allowable tax planning or not. The intention is to assist taxpayers by warning that certain schemes are not valid and to make taxpayers aware of the difference between *'artificial avoidance schemes'* and *'ordinary sensible tax planning'*.

Tax Evasion v Tax Avoidance

Avoidance Scheme number 10 titled 'SDLT staged completion' related specifically to schemes whereby property sales were undertaken in ways intended to avoid SDLT by reducing the purchase price below the SDLT band or threshold. Invariably an intermediate sale, often on the same day, was introduced into the arrangements with the sole intention of removing the true purchase price from tax.

Finally – Property 'Toolkit'

HMRC have placed a range of 20 Toolkits on their website which highlight common errors that have come to HMRC's attention and include steps that can be taken to reduce those errors.

The Toolkits are updated every year and comprise a checklist, explanatory notes and links to further guidance on the topics. Whether to use the Toolkits or not is entirely voluntary.

The one specifically written on property is the 'Property Rental Toolkit' but the following are relevant at various stages of property ownership:

- Business Profits;
- Capital Allowances for Plant and Machinery;
- Capital Gains Tax for Land and Buildings;
- Capital v Revenue Expenditure;
- Inheritance Tax;
- Trusts and Estates.

Property 'Toolkit'

Toolkits can be found at:
www.hmrc.gov.uk/agents/prereturn-support-agents.htm

An error made on a Return could produce a penalty; however, a penalty will not be charged if the taxpayer can demonstrate that he took reasonable care when completing the Tax Return – use of the Toolkit's questionnaire may be proof enough.

Lightning Source UK Ltd.
Milton Keynes UK
UKOW032318140513

210638UK00006B/161/P